A CAGE TO WELCOME

A CAGE TO WELCOME

POEMS

SHANA YOUNGDAHL

STEPHEN F. AUSTIN STATE UNIVERSITY PRESS

For more information:
Stephen F. Austin State University Press
P.O. Box 13007 SFA Station
Nacogdoches, Texas 75962
sfapress@sfasu.edu

Managing Editor: Kimberly Verhines
Book Design: Awele Ilusanmi
Cover Art: Bronwyn Minton
Author Photo: Irvin Serrano

Distributed by Texas A&M Consortium
www.tamupress.com

ISBN: 978-1-62288-951-8

CONTENTS

For my sister, Sonja
And my daughters, Adelaide and Elodie

A CAGE TO WELCOME

FORTY WEEKS

1

First or only?

My child is three—
wakes three times
a night
has no room

I would know. Wouldn't I?

Piling her piss-soaked
blankets on the wood floor
I leave them to fume,

wait for the calendar or the swelling.

2

One day, we'll get serious
about the thing called *trying*.

(If nothing by spring.)

Now a chance to hold the sound
of exhaustion. Open cabinets; line them
with purple jam jars, sweet pickles,
yellow fruit for the body's urges.

3

We rustle.

The day crests
with two bottles of wine empty
by your chair. I'm half-awake.

The air thinks we're
bluebells opening in the rain
but what does it know?

Voices dazzle dawn's soft aches.

I'm nipple aware:
my body holds sunlight.

4

Body is memory.

I bend the night-ocean, howl.

Lying in the cave of youth
our kisses hidden in ski-towers, our hope
a hundred unpregnant snows.

Now this dark autumn.

Winter music in the churchyard: full-throated,
Remember—body—
your own ice.

5

Take this snow in hand. Take the moon
of it. If I feel fresh blood, begin

the task of mourning.
When Julie's mother dies

recall: swimming, warm kitchen tiles.

A town that knows
about mothers. Remember
how quiet blood flows.

6

Start again, open the mouth. Fix the loose board. Close the door.
This is love. Not the body's last chance.

This is livestock, wet-wool, dung, hay-rot; readied to grow.

Think of time, the shards

of death in what we do.

7

In the desert
the birds came
down the chimney
into the damper.

The first time

we lifted the lid
one pulsed, startled skyward.

The second died
cold feet to cold metal.

Dust from line-dried
clothes entered our lungs;
blue sky without song.

8

I know
and don't. I'm half-open
hungry, two days
from late.

I dreamt my name wrong.
I dreamt a boy laughing,
my girl pulling his

yellow booties on, spelling
a name I'd never heard before,
that I could read water.

9

Cells multiply
into someone. Last night

hard frost turned
leaves gold and we know
it happens. We depend

on color. Each
fall the maple's red means
we turn and are
almost home. No matter
where it was
we wanted.

10

Low-tide,
mud arms full of girl
I squint across seaweed,
shovel clams.

After twelve weeks,
less worry. Count
one, two,

we've done this before
three,
we know
four, five

Red tide. Red shells. Don't eat.

Wait. *Six, seven, eight. .*

11

Memory: a valley of
purple flowers.

Sherry said,
  Your first too?

Then died. Hands basketball big. Body
risen like dough.

At the funeral mine cried.

Her husband tried to remember
the baby's name. Pink

Heather. Snow fell
like angels nearing the light.

12

In the deep sea
organisms emit
an unexpected
glow.

Before
they turned off
the machine
giving Sherrie life
they lay the newborn
on her chest, watched
their hearts beat
in time.

Now: a spinal column
thin as webs stretches
inside this tale.

13

Truck collecting trash
causes a gag.

Think stones returning
to water, rippling out.

Words turn vaporous.
I'm poisoned.

Fetus
in ticking space.
Not-yet-the-size-of-a-lemon, not-yet-the-weight-of-a-cat's-head.

I'm a cage to welcome   clinging.

Outside the trees
breathe. Dizzy things.
Don't look.

14

If in this making I am more myself;

The body's grief
is not mine;

the leaf before apple
is not enough; the flower

is what feeds you;

I am mountains, spinning brain-tissue,
rapid multiplication;

I am more God.

15

She knows
the word *harvest* asks,
Mama what color is the sky when it might snow?

I want to extend
the catch of days with three
in the room where small fists
hold the seed, a faith
as great as sparrows.

16

Our web hinges us in dreams.

The daughter screams: *Sleep spiders!*
On my blanket! A pretend spider! See?

Humidifier whirs.

It—what if it—comes back?!

Real biting, made-up spiders.

It will. I know I don't sleep
with my eyes closed.

17

Dream spiders are green.

They will not   go away.
They are in   your dreams too,   also caterpillars.
They're still coming, can't you
see Mama?   Stop them!

At dawn—

Good. Now
there are only trees.

—her feet
on my pillow, cocooned
in sheet.

18

Childhood, my hands, she doesn't want to share.
But I know the sweet
specter of a sister-shadow.
My own secrets shared
in sleep, how my sister whispered
straight to my dream ear.

I can hear everything you say
and what you don't.

19

Already they have secrets:
Daughter under my shirt
lips against me.

What will one give
to the other?

A leaded love
we will not know.

Just as they cannot see
our glistening drink,
our reach for the fruit,
our universe, it's stars.

20

In the dream bodies arch
like hills behind the rain-wet
Alhambra. Monastery
orange trees witness
the howl of hands.
This exhausted fruit
tastes tail-pipe. No
husband to take
my night and walk
sleep-circles, no knife-blade
carefully removing
the peel.

21

While lying
on the floor
next to your sleeping sister
vomiting and crying
in turn, I feel you.
We can't go to the zoo
because her fever grew
to thin fear. And
you, twitching
butterfly, were you
worried too?

22

On Friday we will know
your sex. We explain XX or XY
little dots to your sister
who falls headfirst
to the wood floor. My arms
bring quiet, but all night
my hands remain checking
for breathing, hoping
blood won't steal morning.

23

She, the promise of bulbs buried in fall,

will learn to stand
in our kitchen, make
noodles, feel dough
between her fingers,

will run with her sister
through tented sheets
drying under birches,

will arrive
sudden as daffodils.

24

Here: hold the edge of my dream.

It is a better way
to communicate.

Soon, I will have two daughters

to spit in the dirt, poke sticks in the bee tree.

Now, there is only sky. Breathe in that unreal blue.

25

What if you die when I'm still a little girl?

The usual lie about dwindling honeysuckle, dewy grass,
traceable fox prints, wool, crows and starlings:

a dry shredding to add into memories of palms
rubbing her back when sleeping, of lilac-scented hair.

26

Hands or feet down?
Little prods of midwife.
Punches-or-kick
we're not sure.
She is curled tight

will hang, our hibernating bat,
our sleeping hallowed girl, waiting

for the snows to melt, the first
flowers to come and go.

27

The mud-print of dawn
lifts into light, into
dust, weeping and wasp-needle,
as alarm bells chime.

You can hold light
like this; we walked
to school bare-legged,
March 21 reading
student love letters
in sidewalk chalk like
the archeology of Peru.

28

At the aquarium,
starfish in faux rock pools
stiffen under my touch.

My daughter places
her hand into the tank
where the small sharks swim.

The world of voices
hums with all
the wild races
of the sea.

29

Blood is always forgetting.
See my veins
perennial bruises
on the leg's skin
skirts rise to reveal
spindle blooms that bulge
purple and ache. I wrap legs
at dawn and each night
raise them against the wall
turning the flow back.

30

Names should come from
the earth, ask the books: Rowan and Oriel.

The name a three-word poem
like "fruit-eating bat,"
"white-footed vole,"
"yellow-rumped honeyguide"

or "Rosella in flight"
"ledges echoing laughter,"
"mourning doves rising,"
"water through hair,"
"weeks until birth."

31

Open your eyes underwater
here time is doubled
for lack of air. Look at the stream

of my hands—these lotus-flowers tattoos
appeared one afternoon now

white and pink blossoms wave
down here we are a darkening tree,
rising, we swim.

32

I sleep alone as Husband
battles night.

Dream acid burns the baby's
back,
she is an albino alligator,
possibly dead,
and no one can answer
my questions.

Finally he returns
wet with long work.

Avocado seeds
in our window may sprout.

33

Mainland rich of flies, birchbark
below the seasick-moon
where I move like a marionette
lift painted eggs,
taste mouthfuls of jam, spell
myself sideways.

Hornets calm the animal
caged with bloodied rib and leg-bones,
humming as they clean.

34

These minnows travel and cut
a pharaoh's prophesy.

The baby floats to the hands
of coal-scented fisherwoman.

Oh holy girls whose heads I held
to the ground
weeping, girls who
picked snakes, winnowed bows.

Vernix, this seal
against water
is done for.

35

Thistle. Blackberry in palm
sweet mix of juice and blood.

I'm going now into the forest, toward the river.
Reach out your tree to press me onward:
I will bring back the crying thing. I will show it the dawn.

36

It begins   a blood cramp,
rendered strange after months
of rising
the body
mud-caked, cracking.

Don't warm the water. It's not time.
Drink tea. Eat.
Move or lie still. You are
not a clock. The body
chimes only in warning. Listen.

37

The night air is a merchant.
                    Cover your face.

Find
a stone to fit the palm,

our last iris, photographs of daughter's wet curls, half-burned
                and broken candles, recall when sister

believed the rainbow alive.

Collect your pebbles.

38

I leak
dying larkspur and the strain
of mileage.

It's a glass night,
with clean towels,
and midwives in
the basement room
a pool of water
where spills wet spines
and this damp
brings the cool harness
of crying.

39

We set out walking;
the child grabs a stick
points at clicking marmots
shakes the trees and piñon
bleeds into her fingers
she twists it into her hair.
She is pitched
and dust rises like fire
billowing between sisters.

40

Cooing I am ordered
torn. Baby suck
and blowing birch.
Little night. No
stairs. Oak cradle
is your singing
built and undone
in sleep. Here
you are. Who you are.
Starlings and forsythia
unfold every
hour with you.

Windows

The problem of windows is a problem of daughters.

Windows of oyster, windows of stone, windows of mica
and horn. Latticed windows framed in iron or glass—clear or marbled
that shatters but won't burn. Bow windows and oriels, unglazed,
and lintels of fanned brick grated with wood and metal,

clerestory windows for light and birds and god, specularia
from Spain clear as beaded rain, pointed windows and those that circle

light, with colonnettes or pediments, or movable sashes
for air and light. And daughters. Fan lights and side lights

of plate glass, windows for taxing bricked up
to feed girls grown thin at the table, starving for light.

The daughter's gift: a paned
body. The mother pours open,
becomes a sieve.

Hold the winter child naked
in the sunlit window for
vitamins the breast lacks. Hold
her in the golden light as her
thin hairs rise, as she pales.

Of course, the daughters' room
must have windows and there's
the danger.

Recall: my sister at the window
  asking for money. Cash for gas and cocaine
  all the way to Mexico.

        (forty dollars from the box
        in mother's underwear drawer)

She returns: bearing
a woven green gift-blanket,
sparklers to lite
in the driveway.

Mother at the window
watched hands drop
the threat of fire.

She learns of leaving at the window.
Two is still a shared body; the morning
will not detach her from shoulder or breast.
She craves *one more* until one is gone as if
my work could be only *lift to glass,
point and name*: maple, mulberry, shadow
sun, bicycle and basket. No, I *work*
and leave though she thrusts
body into pane and her screams echo
into the car, down the road, until
I'm wishing the windshield wipers
would wash my wet skin away.

On the first hot day of the season
we open the windows along
the front of the house. Screenless.
My daughter
is lifted through;
she laughs, clambering
between worlds.

We did not build these walls
or install the double panes
to keep you. Did not build

your bodies in warm darkness
as a trap. What we made
with wood, glass, brick, nail; what

we grew in the body by
vitamin, plums, kale
and collard greens was not

asked for. As you grow
you will notice this. When the trap-
that-is-not-a-trap deceives you, daughters,

remember: even Rapunzel found
a way out. For you, it will be easy.

Now, open the window so we hear birds.
Last night you forgot to close the curtains
and the night drifted in. Please,
when you pass through the glass
and into darkness beyond my sight
don't forget the thumbprints
you left. The path
back in. You can slip
silent. If you break through,
you are welcome, but there will
be blood and so much, my darlings,
sweeping and endless wind.

SISTERS

After A Sister Is Language

Sisters lifted in shadow arms shrieking like foot
cut on glass. A wind-wail in the pale forgotten

loam and corners where we pushed dirt to hide. The smallest
home is for sisters where the inked foot

and bonnet rise into late sun. A morning missive
misspoken near the jail shadow of crib rails or looming

parent bed, the tree flutters above newly paved street's stench
where handprints on the desk lamp click off for the whisper

of cotton and the secret shove of elbow-bone-to-belly.
Bellow in the aftermath of noon, amid the climbing vines;

this new kin. This ribbon light in the white-walled room.
A fragment to have and forget, have and forget,

forget and have the hands, the twinned shadow,
the forking comb, that mewling beast; the newest sister.

≈

And what is next? The round vowels of cover-speak,
the word mother knows, mouth of the old country, old tongue
in new mouth, in the flat land, in the heated
room the dolls named and bathed in the cotton mind
where the sisters chant rhymes to lose.
The child walks into the schoolhouse and knows
nothing of the language but speaks
song and rhyme. The mind is memory
of a blue light that can't reach us. Head bowed
in halogen. Lips tight in a vow of forgetting.

That language. Old repeat, of dumb, of doll dress,
of young sisters, teach them
a deep tonic, new words for this dance—

Here is the landscape
for pots and a garden of places I won't follow you, sister.

See: when one is cut the other is crying.
You remember how it was. With us
like it is with them. Like us
as it was for our mother.

Our grandmother? She never saw
her own again. Waved goodbye on a deck
with chipping paint and seagull splatters, she reached
out her arms and stretched out across a long earth.

But even now, if I open my mouth in the twilight I can't find your
noontime, sister.

So I tell them: yes she takes half your things
and yes, you should be thankful.

Imagine if there was only that starched
pillow case. Imagine the empty hollow of her, she will
one day just blow out the window and there will be no
more rocking after that pine-pitch.

You might remember the bark on your legs
how she pulled you up, or how always her hair
was impossibly long and the sting
when she softly clutched you after closing her palm round
a bumblebee and crushing it alive saving

you the swell of it, lavender rubbed and walking
on hot pine needles, what you needed
before you needed.

Your mouth open wide.

My Sister's Memory Is Half My Own

When they found my friend dead
one dawning, we spoke of him
in a red-sweatshirt arms extended
over the wet rocks. That it might
not have been him is the ache I speak
of, after all the empty tissue-boxes
so much is simply the scent of ginkgo leaves,
sidewalks dressed in those tiny golden fans.

We recall him holding his Christmas
candle in a sweater too thick for the weather.
He hugged me then. It may have been the last
time. We can't be sure. Some churches

banish those not revived by the song
of many praying, those who tumble
into the night willingly, but we never believed
in an endless wander. We grew up hiking canyons;
from the bottom there are two ways up, one leads
home, the other deep into mountains. That death
should work differently is unimaginable.

There may be an age when you can understand time,
but only occasionally am I aware of how much
we are losing; we still bathed in the river of feathers
though each year it took a child or two. I can't recall
who, only the men in orange on their way down
and the noise of the helicopters above, ladders
extended in hope of a waving arm.

Between Sisters There is a Small Flower that Crumbles

We held the summer
with our burning fists.
Ran toward the sandbox,
sometimes I climbed
under her long hair, we
learned to raise a tent
at dusk and strike
it by morning. We
did our work like
good children.
When the honeysuckle
dwindled the speckled shadows
provided an afternoon mask
for whatever you were hiding.

In winter when the rare
snow came we were tempted
down the hill with our sleds
we tempted and took
cash from the woolen handbag
in our mother's driveway
we spoke of night. I'd like
to say I am sorry. Wherever
we walked on the lawn, the snow
melted, forsythia bloomed,
and inside I mouthed bad words
into my pillow.

Now, we rise to bake muffins and sweet rolls
pass the mirror, eggs
cracked in the pan,
outside the owls still
feeding, the marks on

your body angry as talons,
cigarette butts filling
the heart-shaped ceramic
box, me above it
pouting in my long
white skirt wispy as all
things gone by.

If we could walk, today,
into the dewy grass
together, now while the children
are still sleeping
below the rattle of motorcycles
is the song of starlings,
and crow caw, while the fox
footprints are still traceable
in the yard. I'd say, "Look sister,
I think I know what you meant,
but it took me too long. It is still
hard to fold blankets
without you. Around
here there is no
wilting, just a dry shred."

Notes

Forty Weeks is a series of poems with word counts limited to 38-42 words, this variable count reflects the average full-term gestation of humans that is usually calculated with a "due date" at 40 weeks from conception (or the best guess at conception). These poems are erasures of free-writes composed during the weeks of my second pregnancy.

5 is in memory of Nancy Prestopino

Windows references the "window tax" in which houses were taxed in England based on the number of windows, as a result people bricked their windows.

Thank you to the following publications where these poems appeared before, sometimes in slightly different versions;

Windows: published in the chapbook *Winter/Windows*, Miel Books 2012
From Forty Weeks:

1, 8, 37, 38, 39: *Wrath-Bearing Tree*

20: *Painted Bride Quarterly*

40: *The Journal*

2 and 4: *Rhino A Poetry Journal*

After A Sister Is Language: *Juked*

Between Sisters Is A Small Flower That Crumbles: *The Lindenwood Review*

This collection took a decade to come together. I am grateful for the support of my family and writing community over this time especially my friends, colleagues and students at The University of Maine, Farmington. Jeffrey Thomson, Kristen Case and Carey Solarno who provided thoughtful notes. Eireann Lorsung for our half-a-life-time and growing friendship in poetry, Audrey Gidman & meg willing whose poetic energy and friendship were a gift when I needed it most. Thanks also to Lindenwood University and the MFA in Writing program where I've found a home, Gillian Parrish you inspire me daily.

My family, Nathaniel Teal Minton, whose devotion as a father allows me time to do this work and whose love has sustained me nearly half my life. Our girls, Adelaide and Elodie, for their cheerleading and inspiration. I could not do this without you. My sister, Sonja, whose memory is half my own and is always there for me. Tove Cat, thanks for keeping my lap warm as I wrote these. We miss you.

ABOUT THE AUTHOR

Poet and Novelist Shana Youngdahl loves helping people embrace the stories they need to tell. Educated at Mills College, The University of Minnesota, and The University of Maine, Shana teaches in the MFA in Writing program at Lindenwood University. The author of the poetry collection *History, Advice and Other Half-Truths* (SFASU Press), as well as several poetry chapbooks, her novel for Young Adults *As Many Nows As I Can Get*, was a Kirkus Best Book of 2019, and a New York Public Library top-ten book of 2019 (Dial/Penguin Teen). Her second novel, *A Catalog of Burnt Objects* is forthcoming. Originally from Paradise, California, Shana currently lives with her family in the greater St. Louis area.

Connect with her online at www.shanayoungdahl.com, twitter @ shanayoungdahl or Instagram @shanayoungdahl

CPSIA information can be obtained
at www.ICGtesting.com
Printed in the USA
JSHW020708200423
40597JS00004B/23